Ireland
INK

Library of Congress
2 0 1 9 9 1 0 4 2 9

BISAC: Writing, Creative Writing, Villain, Antagonist, Character Development, Character Creation
ISBN-13: 978-1-7335011-3-2
ISBN-10: 1-7335011-3-4

SIX SIMPLE STEPS

CRAFTING BADASS ANTAGONISTS

CREATE
A
VILLAIN

BEN IRELAND

Ireland
INK

S3 Formula™ Books

Write Fight Scenes: The Ultimate Guide That Will Wow Your Readers

Build A World: Imagination to Page

Create A Villain: Crafting Badass Antagonists

The S3 Formula: Publish A Book in Six Simple Steps

Write A Book: Fit More Words Into Busy Lives

Other Books by Ben Ireland

Young Adult Fantasy

The Blacksmith Legacy

Billy Blacksmith: The Demonslayer

Billy Blacksmith: The Hellforged

Billy Blacksmith: The Ironsoul

Bleakwood Lore

Urban Fantasy/ Cyberhorror

The Kingdom City Series

Resurrection

Revolt

Short stories

A Dash of Madness

Kissed A Snake

Moments In Millennia

Fairykin

Sanguification

Hi. I'm Ben.

When I'm not working my day job, cooking dinner, playing with LEGO®, or taking care of the kids, I write books. I'm also exhausted most of the time.

As the author of six published novels and three short stories, I'd like to think I know my way around a keyboard. And when I'm creating art, I have one rule: don't produce crap.

There are a lot of ways I try to avoid making low-quality, low-interest work. I don't always succeed. I've written some real stinkers in my day. But if you apply thoughtful analysis and time to your work, you'll have a greater chance of making something worth reading.

One of the many elements that go into (most) novels is the antagonist. The focus in this book is to learn how to better craft a deep villainous antagonist. To be a villain, they should act nefariously (from our perspective). To be deep, a character needs to have a past driving their actions and motivation convincing us why they would continue. Finally we should make sure our villain is unique and doesn't exist just because we need someone to oppose our protagonist.

Let's get started.

Step 1:

Opening Your Toolbox

The difference between not being an author and being an author is writing a book.

That's it.

With self-publishing becoming more accessible than ever, a greater number of people are publishing books. Which is wonderful because many books that would have never seen the light of day now have an opportunity to be read and loved.

But it also means more books are being published that could have used a bit of attention from an editor. But that's why you're here. You have an idea for a story and you want to make sure it has all the elements to give it a chance of rising above the tide. And whether that's the flood of self-published books, or in the eyes of an agent, making sure you are crafting the best book you can will give you a greater chance of being noticed.

Just writing a book sounds simple, but as you get into the thick of writing, you realize there are a lot more moving parts. You need characters, a plot, and a setting.

But when you begin writing them, you realize that every single character is nuanced, has their own way of speaking, their own history. A plot needs to be original and compelling. A location needs to make sense, be accurate, or at least consistent with the world in which you want the story to take place.

When you begin to take into account everything you need to craft an entertaining, moving, important story, it can be as exponentially complex as you make it. Some authors get lost in the weeds of complexity and never make it out.

The good news is that other storytellers have been there before you and can be a useful guide to keep you from losing your way, becoming overwhelmed, or worse: writing something bad.

One of the best tools you have as an author is your brain. As you read books and watch movies, you enjoy some of them and not others. This might not be something you've really considered before. If something sucked, you may have said you hated it and moved on with your life. If something was great, you're willing to share it with anyone that asked. The vital step you must take in becoming a storyteller yourself is to ask: WHY.

> *"The vital step you must take in becoming a storyteller yourself is to ask:* **WHY.***"*

Think about why you liked that character. Think about why that other character was unrealistic and destroyed your suspension of disbelief. Why was that dialogue engaging? Why did that conversation feel stilted and nonsensical? Why did you like that setting? Why did you hate it? Did they really need to have another gunfight on a smoky rooftop? Serious? Did they? Again?? Why did that villain make you shudder and stay up at night? Why was that other villain weak, almost silly? Why did they bother having a conflict at all, when someone could have reasonably walked away?

And as long as you're asking yourself (and better yet, taking notes) WHY, those Netflix marathons really do count as work. As a result, you'll be able to craft a villain that is layered, important, and not only stands as a challenge to your protagonist but will increase the depth of your story.

What Really Matters:

You already possess the best tool to make your stories shine, and your villains memorable. What we're going to do is teach you a few tricks to make sure you're utilizing it to the fullest potential.

Step 2:

Antagonist/Villain

Our focus in this book is to craft a deep villainous antagonist. Let's clear some crap up so we're all on the same page. What's an antagonist? What's a villain? I'll be brief because this is nothing new, and is pretty much available in the dictionary.

An antagonist is basically someone or something that makes our protagonist's life harder. They can be doing it because they hate our protagonist or hate what our protagonist wants to do. It could also be that they're just doing their job, which conflicts with the interests of our protagonist. Like when your wife wants to go to Disneyland—*again*—and you'd like to see Legoland. She's not a villain, she's just wrong.

Antagonists can also be non-human, like the shark in *Jaws* or the birds in *The Birds*; or inanimate, such as the wilderness in survival stories or the rock in *127 Hours*. In many biographies of famous people, the antagonist can be drugs, depression, prejudice. More often we'll see antagonists as individuals or organizations whose goals are contrary to the protagonist. The list is as long as there are things that can get in your way, which are a lot.

A villain is someone who is villainous. They use nefarious means to obtain their goals. Most frequently, examples of simple villains appear in superhero stories or cartoons. Skeletor, Maleficent, Dr. Claw, Zarcon, Cruella De Ville. The villain embodies evil so our protagonist, presumably good, will want to stop them. Their motivations don't have to be deep for the villain to be worth watching. Ranker's top 100 TV villains(1) includes fairly shallow folks such as Shredder (*Teenage Mutant Ninja Turtles* 1987 cartoon) and Skeletor (*He-Man*). Those guys didn't have much definable motivation for why they would jack stuff up every episode, but we kept coming back. And they've lingered in people's memories as something they enjoyed watching.

But we don't want shallow villains. We want *fully-conceived villainous antagonists*.

"If a character wants something, and it means something to them, then we have a compelling character."

So let's talk about WHY those guys fall under the "shallow" side of the scale. Because if we can't figure out the why, we can't emulate it in our story telling. A good place to start is to ask yourself, what does the villain want, and how much does it matter?

Shredder: As far as I could tell from the cartoon, he was simply running a criminal organization. And somehow, he knew Splinter before he became a mutant. Most of what running a criminal organization entails was above my ten-year-old understanding. So the thing I cared about—what mattered to me—was that Shredder wanted to kill the bodacious Ninja Turtles. I loved those guys. So cool! Skateboarding turtles that know ninjutsu! That's insanely cool. They love pizza—*I loved pizza*. Anyone that wants to destroy that must be evil. But you could have replaced that with a robot and achieved the same thing. Which they literally did in a ninja turtles reboot. (2)

Skeletor: He wanted the power of Castle Greyskull so he could rule the universe. That's it. The protagonist coincidentally lives in Castle Greyskull creating the crux of the conflict. (Which makes me wonder if they had universe-controlling power in Castle Greyskull, why they didn't just zap Skeletor into space dust the second time he showed up, but I digress). The entire show was just an elaborate king-of-the-castle game. We didn't get a reason *why* Skeletor wanted power. Was he trying to right a wrong? Rebuild his family by finding them in a different reality? Be strong enough so he never has to suffer again? No. He just wanted power. Fun to watch. Cool looking guy. But absolutely no emotional motivation for his actions.

People in real life get away with being superficial jerks. But usually not in stories.

A villain which is the protagonist is often called an 'anti-hero.' (Because we don't want to call people we like villains. That would be rude.) Anti-heroes tend to live by the philosophy that the ends justify the means. They act in a way that the audience tolerates, even enjoys, because the results are something we'd want to see.

Frank Castle, from Netflix's *The Punisher*, is a fantastic example of a villainous protagonist. What did he want, and how much did it matter? He KNEW murdering people was wrong, but he was only murdering bad people. And he had a good reason to—revenge. And we cared, because HE cared. The events mattered to Frank, and because of that, the audience cared. Frank would break down and cry, missing his family, hating the fight, experiencing post-traumatic stress from the war. He was a deep character, and well-acted, in my opinion. It made his actions count. It made us cheer him on. It made us cry with him.

If a character wants something, and it means something to them, then we have a compelling character. That goes for protagonists as well as antagonists.

What Really Matters:

An antagonistic villain is against the protagonist and is willing to use villainy to thwart their attempts to succeed. Keep in mind that the antagonist has to have some kind of meaningful motivation, which we'll get into shortly.

Step 3:

Who = Why (Mostly)

Where the character is in life provides the backdrop for how they will act. It affords the framework in which the bad guy is able to behave villainously. There are as many different kinds of villains as there are villainous characters, so I've categorized some of the most common archetypes. The purpose of this exercise is to help you recognize the WHY in other villains not listed here. Pick your favorite villain, figure out what their role is, and pay attention to how it guides their villainy.

> *"The purpose of this exercise is to help you recognize the WHY . . ."*

THE PROFITEERING CROOK:

Your average mob boss would fall under this category: Scarface, The Godfather, etc. They have power, money, and people willing to do what they say. They're usually pretty smart and ruthless, which is why they're at the top.

Mama Fratelli from *The Goonies* is a fun example of a crook, though not particularly deep or successful. Her villainy comes from how willing she is to be mean to the Goonies. She has an interesting dichotomy about how important family is to her, while at the same time being horrible to all her children, not least of all Sloth.

One of my favorites is **Johnny Marcone** from the *Dresden Files* series of novels by Jim Butcher. He's named the 'Crime King of Chicago'. He's taken over all the drugs and gun dealing in the city. But when we first hear about Johnny, we learn that he made it his mission to eliminate child trafficking—nobody touches kids in Johnny's Chicago. Immediately this bad guy isn't all that bad. He's almost a hero. But that doesn't stop him from trying to kill Harry Dresden when the opportunity arises. We learn later on that his reasons for protecting kids is closely tied to why Johnny has worked his way up to the top. It makes him deep, relatable, but still very scary.

ABUSIVE CAREGIVERS

There is something terrifying about someone who is supposed to take care of you but abuses that responsibility. Watching someone who is supposed to find support from another but instead receives abuse can be a moving interaction. I feel this category can be broken up in to two commonly seen villains: the Nurturer and the Monarch.

The Nurturer is someone who is intimately related to our protagonist. They are responsible for the welfare of the character, but for reasons of being evil, or crazy, they do not exercise that responsibility. **Carrie's mom** (From the

Stephen King novel, *Carrie*) is a good example. She suffered trauma from a failed marriage and an unfaithful husband. I'm not clear on if her extreme religious views contributed to or resulted from the marriage. She forced her extreme beliefs on her daughter, and as a result, Carrie was socially awkward, and incapable of navigating the real world that her mom was trying to protect her from.

A bad Monarch can be anyone in charge. The challenge with writing a bad monarch is that they are already at the top. Most monarchs you'll see in stories are simply there to maintain power, or they have a sadistic need to make people suffer. **The Sheriff of Nottingham**, for example, took advantage of being in charge while the king was away and used his position to increase taxes on the innocent civilians. The story of *Robin Hood* is great, but the Sherriff, although evil and scary, really didn't have any compelling motivation for his actions beside greed. To make the person in charge really mean something, you need to find what they want and find out why it matters.

THE STUPID GUY IN CHARGE

I think many of us have been subjected to the will of an idiot, who for some reason or another, has risen in the ranks to be your superior. There is a lot of frustration when dealing with someone who doesn't know how to do their job, but we're obligated to listen to them. However, it's very easy to slip into making the character an idiot or a clown. Keep in mind there is a reason why they got the job. Let that come out in your writing. It might be because they know someone, or because they do actually have some level of competence but they're just in over their heads.

> **Walter Peck**, the EPA guy from the 1984 *Ghostbusters*, was undoubtedly a villain; though his motivation seemed to be nothing but forcing the Ghostbusters to follow the law. He didn't have any depth to him other than he was a jerk. But that's also fairly realistic. A lot of people in life who seem to be against us are just doing their job. Like a police officer giving us a ticket. Don't be afraid to use the stupid guy doing their job, but also, don't make him too convenient.

Make sure there is a logical, smooth reason for the person to enter the scene. That said, a cop as a roadblock to a story is effective, but it's unlikely to be a deep character unless you find a way to spend time with them.

A wonderful example of a bad boss is **Michael Scott** from *The Office* (I'm referring to the US version, because it's the only one I've seen). The show was a comedy, so he got away with being goofy. As a bonus, his antics and ineptitude rarely actually risked anyone's safety. But he was deep because he liked his job, liked being in charge, but he also wanted to be liked. That aspect gave his character an air of sadness and relatability. His "Best Boss Ever" mug, which he bought for himself, is symbolic of the deep need he had to be loved for his leadership.

FOLKS THAT GENUINELY THINK THEY'RE DOING THE RIGHT THING

Walter Peck was only "doing the right thing" because it his job was to shut down unlicensed waste disposal units. He didn't think about the morality or consequences of his actions. For someone to move us while they're doing the right thing, they need to have thought about it and come to the decision that this course of action truly is for the best.

It's hard to think of shallow people who think they're doing the right thing, but **The Operative** from *Serenity* comes to mind. First problem is that the character is Joss Whedon's, and he never produces a shallow character if he can help it. The Operative was hunting down people who might upset the order that the Alliance was trying to maintain. He wanted to create peace and was willing to give up his life to help the Alliance achieve that. The Operative was a little unbelievable because he was totally not doing anything for himself; it was all for the greater good. Joss could have spent more time with him convincing me that he would do that. Perhaps it will be better explained in Serenity II. (I can only hope…)

Thanos from the *Marvel* movies is one of my recent favorites. He wants to obliterate half of the universe. *I get that.* People can be very overwhelming. But he's deeper than that. His planet succumbed to overpopulation, and in order to prevent that from happening to anyone else, he has a simple solution: kill half of everything. He has risen an army and has a vast fleet in order to accomplish these goals. He really sees himself as a hero. "The hardest choices require the strongest wills," he says. A wonderful line to justify his megalomaniacal actions.

"For someone to move us while they're doing the right thing, they need to have thought about it and come to the decision that this course of action truly is for the best."

THE SOLDIER

A soldier is someone who is willing to fight for a cause, but it's not just your average joe. This character has been trained to fight. A police officer, a Navy SEAL, a ninja, a gang member.

The Terminator is one of my favorite movies, and one of my favorite villains. But he's literally a robot doing what he's programmed to do. And he's so good at it! He had fantastic aim, knows all about weapons, he fears no one. It makes him horrifying because he is so tough and unrelenting, but he's utterly shallow. (Which is why *Terminator 2* is so, so good. But you'll have to see that to know what I'm talking about).

Inspector Javert from Victor Hugo's *Les Misérables* has a lot of similarities to the Terminator. He is relentless in his pursuit of Jean Valjean, but his programming is coming from a rigid moral code. It's so rigid, he's not able to see that a small crime (stealing loaf of bread) is very different from, say, murder. Any crime makes a man an unforgivable villain. He is so well written that the statement: stealing is equal to murder, which doesn't make logical sense, is completely believable in context with Javert's character. And because Javert is following the law, he perceives himself as the good guy. But because we like Jean Valjean, Javert is a jerk. A compelling jerk.

THE TEACHER

Characters in teaching positions have a lot of power over others. Characters can feel trapped under a teacher with little way to retaliate or escape. It can be a very horrifying, hopeless position. It's important to remember that while some people are simply horrible, mean people, a good villain is more than that. Mean for the sake of mean is realistic, but it has the potential to make your character flat. Teachers make great villains, if you do them right.

Professor Dolores Umbridge from J. K. Rowling's *Harry Potter and the Order of the Phoenix* comes to mind. She used her position as teacher to fulfill her sadistic needs by using banned 'punishment' techniques. She had deep rooted prejudices that manifest themselves in her treatment of half-breed magical creatures and mudbloods. She grew up ashamed of her half-blood heritage, and it ended up defining who she was and her whole magical career. But despite the reasons given for why Umbridge was so hateful, the book never justified her actions.

Pai Mei in *Kill Bill* is the Kung-Fu master tasked with training our protagonist, Kiddo, to become a mighty warrior. If he counts as a villain depends entirely on who you ask. To Kiddo, he was a good teacher who used strict discipline and unyielding rules to inspire her to reach her full potential. And he was a hard-ass. Her hands sore from punching planks of wood all day, Kiddo can't use her chopsticks and resorts to picking up her rice with her fingers. Pai Mei asks if she's a dog and throws her rice on the floor to eat like a dog. Kiddo then picks up the chopsticks and starts to eat "properly," which pleases Pai Mei. I personally would not have responded well to such treatment. To Elle Driver, another student of Pai Mei, he was a horrible, oppressive force. She struggles against his teaching style until they reach a point where Pai Mei plucks out her eye to discipline her. That's cool because we hate Elle. But yanking someone's eye from their socket is not a nice thing to do by any standard. If a teacher is villainous can have a lot to do with the temperament of the student.

THE PSYCHOPATH
(SPECIFICALLY, THE PSYCHOPATHIC KILLER)

The text-book version of a psychopath isn't often what you'll see on the screen. A true psychopath is generally manipulative and self-centered, and has a distain for the rules. By this definition, Jordan Belfort from *The Wolf of Wall Street* is closer to a psychopath than most "psychopathic" characters you'll see or read about. Being a psychopath doesn't mean they're willing to murder people.

The way many authors use 'psychopaths' as characters is someone who kills others. Yet the murders are not always selfish. Some authors have used the mindset of one who is emotionally detached and does not feel remorse, to serve the greater good—at least the good from the perspective of the character.

Psychopathic villainous antagonists are difficult to give a motivation beyond 'they're just crazy'. There have been a few which have caught the imagination over the years (such as the characters in *The Silence of the Lambs*. Though that could be a paper on its own). The challenge with writing "psychopaths" is to portray deep motivation when the character is so removed from reality. It really boils down to giving them motivation that us normies can get behind.

In the anime, *Death Note*, a teenager **Yagami Light** finds a magical notebook. When he writes someone's name in the notebook they die. The premise sounds a little silly, but it's one of the coolest animes I've seen. It was fascinating to watch a brilliant student suddenly be given the power to arbitrarily kill. The result is a moral tailspin as he becomes more and more willing to take life at whim. While not strictly a psychopath, it's a great example of how power—and the idea that he will never get caught—corrupts Yagami. He's the protagonist, so we're rooting for him. But as he feels closer to being caught, his actions becoming increasingly villainous, and less justifiable.

The television show *Dexter* is a lot of fun. The protagonist is not quite a psychopath, and papers have been written analyzing him trying to decide where he falls. But the point is he is a serial killer who kills criminals—cleaning up the messes the cops can't legally handle.

Though the real criminals were the writers for seasons five through eight. Just kidding.

The season that stands out to me is season four where they introduce **Arthur Mitchell**. Mitchell is a serial-killer without a code dictating whom he should not kill. As a killer, he can see Dexter for who he is, and threatens to destroy the life Dexter has built for himself. He makes such a compelling villain because he is a mirror of our protagonist and is able to outmaneuver him. His intimate knowledge of our protagonist, and his willingness to kill anyone he chooses, makes him terrifying.

What Really Matters:

There are as many kinds of villains as there are villainous characters. Figure out where the villain is in life at the beginning of the story so their actions to stop the protagonist make sense and are meaningful.

Step 4:

Villainous Antagonists

So we know what an antagonist is, and we've taken a brief look at the multitude of villains out there. Let's get to what brought us here in the first place: villainous antagonists—a villainous person who is dead-set on stopping our protagonist.

You'll often hear the saying: nobody sees themselves as the villain.

I disagree. Vehemently.

If you immediately put all your villains in this one bucket, you're denying a lot of depth that your villain could have. While it is certainly true that some folks don't know they're the bad guys, many do. The key—and the emotional depth— is that the character *justifies* their actions.

Mob bosses, for example, KNOW they're bad guys, but they justify it by telling themselves they are protecting their family, their business, or their interests. Most people have a conscience and know that hurting people is a bad thing to do. But they have a really good reason for doing it. Without that reason, why would they continue?

> *"The key—and the emotional depth—is that the character justifies their actions."*

SOME PEOPLE JUST LIKE POWER

Examples: Skeletor *(He-man)*, Jafar *(Aladdin)*, Lex Luther *(Superman – though it depends on the version)*, Emperor Palpatine (Star Wars)

This is a pretty boring reason to be a villain, though it's probably the most common. It's a lot of work to get to the top (I assume. I haven't risen to the top of my villainous organization yet), and people don't want to lose the advantage which they have gained. The key to making a compelling villain that wishes to maintain their power is highlight how they got it. Sure Trump-like rises to power happen where the person neither deserves nor knows how to handle the power they have. But if you want the villain to

have a reason to fight, make them afraid of what they stand
to lose.

SOME PEOPLE THINK THEY HAVE A RIGHT TO BE VILLAINOUS

Examples: Jordan Belfort *(Wolf of Wall Street)*, Your boss *(At work)*, King Theron *(Billy Blacksmith)*, The Joker *(Batman – The Animated Series)*, Syndrome *(The Incredibles)*, Mr. Glass *(Glass)*

Folks who think they are smarter than others or better than others will assume they have something to offer the world that the world would be stupid to reject. I see this frequently as the basis for real-world conflict. It is creatively easy for a character who thinks they're right to have a well-defined motivation. The challenge would be to make it an interesting motivation. Be careful of motivations we see frequently: fighting for the sovereignty of their country or fighting for religious reasons. I'm not saying avoid those motivations, but make sure they are crafted well so the audience isn't left saying 'not this again.'

SOME PEOPLE ARE PROTECTING THEMSELVES OR OTHERS

Examples: Dexter *(Dexter),* **Thanos** *(MCU),* **Khan** *(Star Trek)*

This motivation is a wonderful one for giving someone a reason to fight. Most of us care about someone, so it's easy to put our character in the position where the individual or individuals they care about are in danger. People will fight mercilessly and violently to protect those they love.

> *"But if you want the villain to have a reason to fight, make them afraid of what they stand to lose."*

SOME PEOPLE ARE JUST DOING THEIR JOB

Examples: Walter Peck *(Ghostbusters),* **Krios** *(Billy Blacksmith)*

Often people are simply doing their job. But when it comes down to fighting for their job, a lot of people will decide that self-preservation is more important. If someone is doing their job, and you want them to stand their ground when presented with a challenger, they need to believe in their job. That's the difference between a guard who will drop their gun at the first sign of trouble and one that will dig in and defend their place of work.

What Really Matters:

Villains are people, too. They don't have to cackle manically as lightning strikes outside the lab window—unless that makes sense. Bad people who know they're bad will justify their actions. Bad people who don't know they're bad will have a good reason for their actions. But if they love someone in danger, or they believe in their work, they will fight for it.

Step 5:

It's EASY To Define Our Villain By the Protagonist – Don't.

A common mistake with first time story tellers is that they'll come up with a protagonist, and an adventure, then tack on the antagonist because the protagonist needs something to get in their way.

Don't do that.

If you have a warrior that needs to steal a magical crystal from a castle, don't just throw any old wizard in there to fight her. Throw a deep, well-conceived, wizard for your warrior to kill. It will make that fight that much more meaningful. Sure, some folks just love brawling, but that makes them a bro, and nobody cares about bros. Here are some key points to keep in mind when crafting your villain.

- **The villain existed before (sometimes) our protagonist.** They didn't spontaneously appear in the castle in front of the crystal. Unless they literally did, and that's the only space in time you've given to the villain. If you put no thought into how they got there, the reader is going to be able to sense that. Cardboard characters aren't just flat, they *taste* like cardboard.

- **The villain has their own life.** Is she married? Does she have kids? Is he doing this just for the money? Does he believe in the king that told him he is needed to protect the magical crystal? Is the armor he has to wear day in-day out while standing guard uncomfortable? Is she working on a novel to pass the time? When our protagonist appears in the villain's life, they probably already had a dozen things on their mind. Will the destruction of the -inator get in the way of their alimony hearing? Probably. We don't need to know all the details, but there are probably other things keeping the villain up at night. At least before the protagonist becomes a thorn in their side.

- **The villain has their own journey to get where they are.** Has she been tirelessly working her way up in the ranks? Is she in her magical lab working on the philosopher's stone, fulfilling her life-long dream of being an alchemist, when suddenly our protagonist busts down the door? The little details will shine through as you write. Even if you are the only one who sees them all, it's important that they exist. If she doesn't care about the room, she'll start throwing vials at the protagonist. But if her life's work is in there, she is going to do everything in her power to minimize the damage whilst protecting her sanctuary.

- **The villain has their own reasons to stay/leave/change where they are.** This part can be where the protagonist and villain most closely intermingle. If the villain is trying to keep the kingdom the way it is, naturally our protagonist wants it to change. If the villain wants to leave, our protagonist is fighting against the devastation that will cause. Once you know why the villain is where they are in life, you'll be able to figure out where they want things to go from there—and naturally, why our protagonist respectfully disagrees.

What Really Matters:

The villain was a child at some point. They did interesting things to get to where they are. They have hopes and dreams. They have that job for a reason. And if they're fighting to stop the protagonist, chances are they're not just there for the money. (Or they are there just for the money. Because people love money.)

Step 6:

Get to Know Your Villain

Like we just discussed, your villain can't exist just because your protagonist needs someone to stop them. Your villain needs to be someone you can picture, someone you might even care about. To do that you have to ask yourself: who are they, and what do they want?

WHO ARE THEY?

A great place to start is to follow the pointers from the section above. You spend months (at least) dreaming about your protagonist—the villainous antagonist deserves the same respect. If the villain is a main character, you need to give them the attention you would give any main character. Do that however you like. Make a character sheet. Write chapters from their perspective. Write love letters as the villain. Whatever you need to do to understand them as well as you do your protagonist. Their conflict will naturally be more layered and intense as a result. Tacking on a tragic backstory because you suddenly realize they need one will rarely result in the villain's actions and motivations being consistent across every page on which they appear.

WHAT DOES THE VILLAIN WANT?

Real-life villains tend to do things just because they feel like it. It's realistic, but it's boring. We can count on the actual people you meet to be complete jerks just because they can *looks at most of the bosses I've ever had*. If you want your villainous character to move the audience and stay with them, haunt them even, then you need to give them deep, real, meaningful motivation. Shredder and Skeletor are "cool" villains, but there is no meat to their motivations. Their entire appeal is the fact that they're willing to stand up to cool heroes. There is a sort of bravery in that, and I respect their tenacity, but it's dull, creatively speaking.

The key to creating a villain that can move audiences is to give them something to care about. What problem were they hoping to solve by turning to a life of crime? What evil are they trying to stop through murdering people? Without a driving influence on their actions, villains will just be criminals; flat and boring. Your hero probably went through a life-changing experience at some point that made them choose to stand up and fight, (and even if they didn't, I think you know what I'm talking about). What happened to your villainous antagonist that changed them, pushed them over the edge to commit heinous deeds, or even changed their focus so they suddenly had a reason to continue being a criminal? What happened to give their life purpose? Take Batman for example. When his parents were shot it motivated him to fight crime. What if it motivated him to control crime instead? (I think this actually happens in one of the alternate storylines, but holy research, Batman, the Batman Wikipedia page is HUGE.)

GET TO KNOW THE VILLAIN – BUT DON'T LET THEM GET AWAY WITH MURDER

Too often I have seen bad guys become so loved that their villainy is kind of shrugged off because we like them now.

Don't do this.

You will be letting your audience down.

People love villains, they love good villains, villains with color and purpose and drive and motivation. But rarely will an audience be left satisfied when the villain gets away with their criminal acts. I think that's why the ending of *Breaking Bad* was so satisfying, and the end of *Dexter* was not.

If you think Walter White was a hero for his actions in *Breaking Bad*, then you're probably not in a position to write a convincing hero. You could write about villains all day, though you probably wouldn't realize it.

Superficially, *Breaking Bad's* Walter White began manufacturing methamphetamine to help pay for his medical bills to cover the cost of his cancer treatment because getting sick in the USA is a horror story all on its own. But his character was so much deeper. He did it as an eff-you to the system that had screwed him over. And it seemed as a sort of revenge against the universe for giving him the short end of the stick. What made it so compelling was that he used his wasted genius to create the best meth anyone had ever seen. As the story begins, he enlists the aid of Jessie Pinkman. But he soon begins manipulating and using the younger man for his own selfish wishes. Jessie was pretty much a nobody at the beginning and soon becomes trapped in the self-destructive vortex Walter generates. The sacrifice that Walter

White makes in the end to rescue Jessie is fulfilling and satisfying. Walter gets what he deserves, and he does one last good deed.

Dexter was not satisfying. The premise of a serial killer that only kills serial killers is intriguing, and for about four seasons they did a great job keeping the show interesting. But they fell victim to what so many long-running series fall victim to. They end up being nice to almost every single character, whether they deserve it or not. Dexter is a serial killer. He's killed a lot of people in his life. A LOT. And some of the people he's killed didn't strictly deserve to be killed. He had a rigid code dictating who was supposed to die which he failed to follow on several occasions. Thus, by his own rules, *Dexter deserved to die*. The Rotten Tomatoes review of Dexter succinctly states: "The darkly dreaming *Dexter* lays to rest once and for all in a bitterly disappointing final season that is so hesitant to punish its anti-hero for his misdeeds, it opts to punish its audience instead."(3)

I want you to note the specific way that was stated: If you don't punish those that deserve to be punished, you are punishing your audience.

"If you don't punish those that deserve to be punished, you are punishing your audience."

Of course there are exceptions to every rule, but if you are going to write a villainous antagonist, give them deep purpose and distinct personality traits, then you need to be brave enough to give them one last thing: what they deserve.

People may say they hope the bad guy gets away, but if they don't, the ending will be as satisfying as chocolate and coffee on a snowy winter evening.

What Really Matters:

Get to know the villain. Understand what they want. But never, ever, ever, let them get away with villainy. Unless it makes sense in the narrative for the villain to escape justice, the audience wants the bad guy to receive their due.

My editor says this book needs a conclusion, but I've already told you everything I want you to know. Take time with your work, enlist the aid of trusted friends to read over your infantile manuscripts. If you truly trust them, listen to what they say. Don't produce crap. If you read something you've written and you think it's crap, write it again.

Spend time with your villains. They have feelings, too. Horrible, evil feelings, but feelings nonetheless. And never be afraid to give them what they deserve, no matter how much you love them. Justice will always be satisfying to your reader.

And stay hydrated. Drinking enough water is underrated for general wellbeing.

References:

1. https://www.ranker.com/crowdranked-list/best-tv-villains-of-all-time
2. https://en.wikipedia.org/wiki/Teenage_Mutant_Ninja_Turtles_(2014_film)
3. https://www.rottentomatoes.com/tv/dexter/s08

BEN IRELAND: THE DEFINITIVE BIO

Ben Ireland was born in Melbourne, Australia—too late to be an 80's kid, and too early to be a Millennial—he grew up in what is known as the Artax Generation. Transplanted to Houston, Texas when he was 17, Ben officially has no idea where he belongs in the world. Except now he lives in Utah with his rock-star wife and above-average children, so things seem to be working out. He studied psychology at the University of Houston some time in the early 2000s, and thus has enjoyed a long career in IT.

Ben is a multi-genre award-winning writer of both Young Adult Urban Fantasy and Cyber-Horror. He made up the genre cyber-horror because he doesn't know where Kingdom City fits. But that sounds right. Ben received the Gold Quill 2017 for Billy Blacksmith: The Demonslayer from the League of Utah Writers. His other Blacksmith Legacy books include

Billy Blacksmith: The Hellforged, Billy Blacksmith: The Ironsoul, and Bleakwood Lore. Kingdom City Resurrection and Revolt are awesome, but book 3 is on hiatus. He has published several short stories—all of them good.

You can learn more about Ben and his work at BenIrelandBooks.com.